Original title:
Tropical Skies Above

Copyright © 2025 Creative Arts Management OÜ
All rights reserved.

Author: Sophia Kingsley
ISBN HARDBACK: 978-1-80581-570-9
ISBN PAPERBACK: 978-1-80581-097-1
ISBN EBOOK: 978-1-80581-570-9

Cascading Colors of the Orient

In a realm where colors clash,
Lemons dance and mangoes splash.
Cherries giggle in the breeze,
While orange cats pretend to sneeze.

Parrots squawk a silly tune,
Painting rainbows 'neath the moon.
Fruits compete in a loud race,
Chasing shadows, just for grace.

Serene Reflections on Sapphire Waters

Fish don hats and strut around,
Mermaids laugh, no care is found.
Crabs wear glasses, think they're cool,
While seaweed sways like a school.

Bubbles pop with giggles bright,
Sardines planning a fishy flight.
Otters slide with giggling flair,
While dolphins play with sand in hair.

The Glow of Serendipity at Dusk

Fireflies in a dance unite,
Twinkling stars decide to fight.
Cicadas play their evening song,
While critters party all night long.

Moonbeams swirl, a restless tide,
With noiming mice who love to glide.
Laughter echoes through the night,
As shadows join the silly flight.

Daybreak Promises and Midnight Whispers

Sunrise tiptoes with a grin,
Sunflowers cheer as day begins.
Coffee cups and muffins cheer,
While sleepy bears snooze near the pier.

Night comes wrapped in starry tales,
With crickets chirping silly gales.
Owls give winks, quite unimpressed,
As sleepyheads remain unguessed.

A Horizon Painted with Laughter

The sun wears shades, oh what a sight,
Fluffy clouds giggle, floating bright.
Seagulls squawk jokes, dive with flair,
The beach ball bounces, flying in air.

Waves roll in, with a playful splash,
Sandcastles topple, oh what a crash!
Footprints giggle, telling tales of fun,
Under this giggle, we'll dance in the sun.

Echoes of the Calm Sea

The ocean hums a silly tune,
Shells tap dance beneath the moon.
Jellyfish waltz with arms so wide,
A crab in shades takes joy in stride.

Surfboards laugh, they catch a wave,
Turtles joke, oh how they behave!
The tide rolls in with a cheeky grin,
As sand crabs clap, let the fun begin.

Enchanting Nightfall in Paradise

Stars twinkle bright, wearing tiny hats,
Fireflies dance, oh look, they chat!
Laughter floats on the evening breeze,
While palm trees sway with joyful tease.

Moonlight spills like a glowing drink,
Under a sky where the crickets wink.
A hammock sways as the night takes hold,
Beneath a canopy of glittering gold.

The Glow of Twilight's Embrace

Marigold whispers with a cheeky spin,
The sunset chuckles, let the fun begin.
Colors collide in a silent joke,
As laughter blends with the softening smoke.

As night kisses day, what a funny sight,
Stars wearing costumes, shining so bright.
Each shimmering glow tells a whimsical tale,
In a world where laughter will never fail.

Soft Hues of Evening's Caress

The sun dips low, in blush and gold,
A parrot laughs, it's time to scold.
Flip-flops squeak as folks stroll by,
They dance like fish—oh my, oh my!

Coconuts roll, a merry chase,
Chasing shadows, just in case.
The sunset winks, a cheeky tease,
While laughter floats on evening breeze.

Majestic Light Over Swaying Palms

A lizard struts with quite the flair,
Wearing shades, without a care.
The palms sway slow, as if to rhyme,
With crickets chirping, keeping time.

The moon peeks in, a ghostly grin,
While toucans gossip, natter, spin.
A hammock swings, it's quite the show,
Where dreams of flies and naps do grow.

A Kaleidoscope of Gentle Breezes

A breeze brings tales from distant lands,
Whispers of coconuts in bands.
With giggles hidden in the sand,
Each grain a star, oh isn't it grand?

A crab in shorts, what a delight!
He scuttles fast, a funny sight.
The sun plays tag, a fiery sprite,
While seashells clink in pure delight.

Dreamscapes Beneath Glimmering Stars

Stars tumble down with joyful cheer,
Beneath their gaze, we sip our beer.
A dolphin jumps, a playful tease,
He seems to laugh, 'Come dance with ease!'

The night's a canvas, streaked with fun,
Painted bright by the laughing sun.
Each twinkling light, a cheeky wink,
In dreamscapes vast, we laugh and drink.

Journey through the Glistening Canopy

Swinging vines and buzzing bees,
A monkey steals my fruity tease.
With every step, I feel the sway,
These silly vines just want to play.

Lizards laugh and birds do sing,
A parrot dreams of flying bling.
I trip on roots, then jump with glee,
Who knew the jungle knew of me?

The sun peeks through with a cheeky grin,
While ants throw parties, I just spin.
I dance with shadows, wild and free,
In this green circus of jubilee.

At last, I've reached the riverbend,
Splashing about just like a friend.
Nature's giggles fill the air,
What a joy, this wild affair!

Chasing Shadows Under Radiant Nights

The moon plays hide-and-seek with me,
While crickets join the jamboree.
Bats swoop low, but I don't fret,
With disco lights from stars, you bet!

A firefly winks, 'Come dance with us!'
In this lush garden, there's no fuss.
I twirl between the gleaming trees,
And jump to catch the evening breeze.

Coconut drinks in hand we sway,
While owls hoot, 'It's time to play!'
The night's a canvas, wild and bright,
Where mischief burbles with delight.

As shadows chase and giggles race,
I trip and fall, oh what a place!
Yet every stumble feels so right,
In this soft glow of radiant night.

Feathered Dreams in the Equatorial Hearts

Fluffy parrots in a row,
Squawking tales of toys and dough.
A toucan sports a zany hat,
While dancing like a feathery cat.

A plucky pigeon struts the ground,
With swagger wiggles all around.
He claims the crown, then takes a bow,
'It's easy being cool, oh wow!'

An eagle soars and drops a wink,
To chat with frogs beside the sink.
Together busting out some moves,
In this wild land where all improves!

But when the sun begins to dive,
The party shifts, oh how they thrive!
Birds in pajamas, blissful snore,
Dreaming of adventures to explore!

The Parchment of Dusk

As day retreats, a painted scroll,
Whispers of laughter, fills the whole.
The sun drips down, like melted cheese,
In lazy hues, it aims to please.

An iguana grins, all laid-back,
While crabs do crab walks on a track.
I join their team, we prance around,
Stumbling, grinning, joy abound.

The sky's a canvas, sparks of fun,
With silly shapes, like bolts that run.
Each quirky cloud begins to tease,
A parade of thoughtless, funny ease.

Then dusk arrives with a giggling sigh,
As fireflies dance and dreams comply.
In this parchment of fading light,
We embrace the humor of the night!

The Gentle Strum of a Silken Sky

Beneath the clouds, a ukulele strums,
Birds dance around, singing in their drums.
A squirrel wears shades, looking oh so cool,
While ants do the limbo, in nature's school.

A breeze whispers secrets, it's quite the tease,
As crabs hold a concert, rocking to the breeze.
The sun takes a bow, with a wink and a grin,
While frogs join the chorus, letting the fun begin.

Lizards are DJ-ing, spinning on the grass,
While turtles line up, hoping to be last.
Jellyfish waddle by, in a winky parade,
In this upbeat fiesta, no one's afraid.

So let's strum along, with laughter and cheer,
In this whimsical world, there's nothing to fear.
Under a canvas, painted bright and clear,
Nature's silly orchestra brings us all near.

A Tapestry of Sun and Night

In the daylight's dance, where shadows play,
Roosters wear sunglasses, declaring their sway.
While sunflowers gossip with bees buzzing loud,
The daisies throw petals, they're quite the crowd.

At dusk they all gather, with a wink and a smile,
Crickets in tuxedos, they charm with style.
Fireflies flicker, throwing a glow,
As raccoons tap dance, putting on a show.

The moon tosses glitter, like confetti from above,
As owls get the groove started, all sing of love.
With cats as the judges, on this lively spree,
They score every act with a soft, furry glee.

So in this patchwork of bright, silly delight,
Common critters become stars of the night.
With laughter and music, friendships are tight,
A tapestry woven with joy, pure and bright.

Pirouettes Under the Moonlit Palms

In the moon's soft glow, where the wild things twirl,
Lizards dance boldly, ready to unfurl.
Palm trees are clapping, leaves rustling in glee,
While snails take their time, they're the VIPs.

Crabs in their shells, with a cha-cha flair,
Join a salsa party, without a care.
The frogs leap about, with leaps and with bounds,
While butterflies flutter, spreading joy all around.

Chameleons switch hues, for a change of attire,
While shadows embrace, revealing the mire.
All creatures alive take a turn on the floor,
In this whimsical dance, who could ask for more?

So twirl and groove under those palms up high,
And let laughter echo, like stars in the sky.
In this wild, funny fest, we all feel alive,
A grand celebration where joy will thrive.

Embracing the Warmth of Sultry Nights

In the hush of the evening, as stars appear,
A gecko hums softly, "Let's have some cheer!"
Coconuts roll by, on a slow, lazy quest,
While pelicans gossip, they're truly the best.

Beneath velvet skies, each critter takes flight,
Bathtubs become pools, for a swim in moonlight.
Crickets are strumming on leaves, just for fun,
While raccoons hold court, saying, "We've just begun!"

A breeze carries giggles, tickling the night,
As fireflies giggle, with their flickering light.
Even the stars join in, twinkling and bright,
Inviting all who wander to dance in their sight.

So embrace the warmth, let your spirit unwind,
In this silly night circus, joy's all you'll find.
With laughter and merriment, let's lift up our heart,
In the vibrant embrace, may we never part.

Luminescent Tropics and Solstice Nights

Lizards in shades of day-glow green,
Swaying like they're on a fun unseen.
Coconuts fall from heights with a thud,
Watch out below, it's the fruiting flood!

Giggling crabs dance on the shore,
Pinching toes, always wanting more.
They wave their claws like happy flags,
While seagulls swoop down, it's a comic gag!

The Rhythm of Raindrops and Breeze

Raindrops tap dance on palm fronds high,
Each splash a giggle, a joyful sigh.
The breeze tells secrets, tickles your ear,
Whispers of mischief — oh dear, oh dear!

Dancing in puddles, splashing with glee,
Frogs join the party, come hop with me!
The sun peeks out with a wink and grin,
Turns rain into laughter — let the fun begin!

Hues of Joy on Verdant Shores

Beach balls bouncing, a vibrant spree,
Mismatched sandals dance by the sea.
Colors explode like a piñata popped,
Laughter erupts as the cold waves plopped.

Seashells gossip, trading their tales,
While the sun beats down like old mail trails.
Under the shade, we sip from coconuts,
Sharing dad jokes and rib-tickling cuts!

Mystic Mornings and Sunset Reveries

At dawn, the roosters crow in duet,
While sleepy-eyed sunflowers just fret.
The coffee brews with a fragrant cheer,
Dances of dreams as the morning draws near.

As day slips to dusk, colors ignite,
Fireflies flicker, oh what a sight!
Chasing their lights, we stumble and trip,
Laughter echoes on our evening trip!

Wings of Change Beneath Stardust

A parrot wore a crown of gold,
Chasing dreams that never grow old.
He squawked of treasures far and wide,
While sipping juice with feathered pride.

A monkey swung with comic grace,
Belly laughs in a vibrant race.
He tripped on vines, oh what a sight,
Fell in the pond, causing a fright!

The toucan donned a silly hat,
Announced, "I'm off to conquer that!"
He flapped but fell, all in good jest,
As fruit bats cheered, he tried his best.

Through giggles shared, the night took flight,
In banter wrapped, the world felt right.
With wings of change, we drift and soar,
Laughing beneath a cosmic door.

Reflections of Day's End in Parady

A crab with shades sat in the sand,
Played tunes that made the crowd expand.
With each pinch of claw, he danced away,
His moves inspired, brightened the day.

The sun winked low, painted the sea,
As fish flicked tails, laughing with glee.
They splashed about, a fin-tastic team,
In the water, they shared a dream.

A pelican with snack-filled cheeks,
Swooped down fast, gave playful shrieks.
Snack attack! He dropped a few,
And laughed at all the mess he knew.

As daylight closed with a golden thread,
Laughter lingered in the air like bread.
In Parady's heart, joy took its stand,
Reflections sparkled across the sand.

The Allure of a Glistening Evening

A firefly danced with twinkling charm,
Lighting up flowers without a qualm.
"Catch me if you can!" it teased with glee,
But bumped a tree and fell into a spree!

The iguanas played their nightly games,
Wearing sunglasses, calling out names.
They pranced about, with style so bold,
Chasing shadows in the dusk of gold.

The breeze brought tales from oceans far,
Tales of sandcastles and a hidden star.
With giggles shared, the night grew bright,
As stars joined in, lending their light.

In that glistening, cheeky retreat,
We laughed aloud, with mischief replete.
The evening sang with a playful refrain,
A night to remember, once again!

Twilight's Caress on Rustling Leaves

A raccoon donned a shiny waistcoat,
Snuck snacks from a tiny boat.
"I'm a pirate!" he claimed with pride,
Grabbing treats, then took a ride.

Beneath the leaves, a rabbit hopped,
With oversized ears that bobbed and flopped.
His carrot treasure glowed like gold,
As he danced with joy, oh so bold!

The clouds giggled, changing their shape,
A dapper dolphin, hippo, and tape.
Each one squeaked out sweet, silly rhymes,
As twilight played with ticklish times.

In rustling leaves, we found our zest,
Fun and folly at nature's fest.
With twilight's caress, laughter grew wide,
A night of jests and joy to abide.

Celestial Canvas of Coastal Winds

Balloons float high in the warm, soft air,
Kites dance wildly, without a care.
Seagulls squawk, a feathery band,
Stealing fries from a sunbather's hand.

Sunscreen slathers and slips on toes,
A flip-flop war, nobody knows.
A crab in the sand gives a sassy glare,
Thinking he owns that beachside fair.

Children's laughter, a cheerful sound,
Chased by waves, with sand all around.
They build castles, their fate's quite grim,
As water rushes, their hopes swim.

Yet, under the umbrella, we all unite,
Sharing stories, to our heart's delight.
As the sun dips down and the day turns night,
We joke, we laugh, all feels just right.

Lush Horizons Beneath the Sun

Fruits in hand, we stroll the sand,
Sipping coconuts, life feels grand.
Umbrella drinks with tiny straws,
Contemplating folks and their flip-flop flaws.

Palm trees sway, with vibes so chill,
In Bermuda shorts, we laugh at will.
A picnic blanket, a wobbly dance,
Until sighted a dog in a sunscreen trance.

The beach ball flies, a crazy arc,
A headshot! An unexpected lark!
Sun hats tilted, shades askew,
An impromptu fashion show for the view!

Golden rays begin to fade,
While stories of blunders are happily made.
As the sun dips down, we grin with glee,
Life's a beach, both wild and free.

Waves of Serenity and Starry Twilight

As daylight wanes and stars take flight,
The ocean whispers, it feels just right.
Crickets chirp in a tune less known,
We roll on towels, far from home.

The waves crash loud, a raucous cheer,
While jellyfish float, we hold them dear.
A snorkel mask worn as a goofy hat,
We take selfies with a lovable cat.

Flipped burgers and laughter fill the air,
Someone spills ketchup, just a bit of flair.
Umbrellas close, but the fun will stay,
In hearts so light, we dance away.

As we watch the moon take center stage,
Each goofy moment, a page by page.
The night's alive with flickers and bright,
Our laughter echoes, oh what a sight.

Aquamarine Reflections at Dusk

The water gleams, a shimmering show,
With floating ducks that strut just so.
A raccoon sneaks fries from a picnic stash,
While dolphins flip, giving quite the splash.

Fishermen argue over the catch of the day,
As wind in their hair makes them sway.
Sunset paints colors, oh so absurd,
One claims he saw a flying bird!

Sandy toes and water fights,
With wacky hairstyles, pure delights.
As the sun sinks low, we gather near,
Swapping tales while sipping on beer.

Under twinkling lights, the laughter climbs,
With silly jokes and playful rhymes.
Until the stars come out to play,
We cherish the fun of another day.

Paradise Found in the Celestial Vast

In the land where coconuts dance,
The sun takes its daily prance,
Birds wearing shades wing on by,
Laughing loudly, oh my, oh my!

Palm trees sway with a cheeky grin,
As crabs strut about, trying to win,
Sea lions sunbathe, flexing their might,
While the fish are spitting jokes, oh what a sight!

A toucan gives a comedic speech,
While surfers try, but can't quite reach,
A wave that tosses them in delight,
Splashes of giggles under moonlight.

Under the stars, the air is tight,
With laughter echoing into the night,
It's paradise found, what a surprise,
In this whimsical world of delightful skies!

Beneath the Umbrellas of Heaven

Beneath the umbrellas where seagulls squawk,
Sandy toes shuffle and flip-flops talk,
Kids build castles, or just throw sand,
While ice cream drips from every hand.

A crab in a hat leads a parade,
While beachgoers join in, not afraid,
To dance like awkward flamingos might,
In the shade where laughs take flight.

As waves come in with a whoosh and a splash,
A determined dog makes a wild dash,
He's fetched a beach ball, now it's gone,
As the sun sets, the fun carries on!

With cool drinks served on a wobbly table,
Tales get taller, howling, and stable,
Beneath the umbrellas, joy's always near,
With laughter echoing loud and clear!

Iridescent Moments at Sundown

As the sun dips low, colors explode,
Two parrots argue on their load,
'This branch is mine!' they squawk and chime,
While the horizon blushes, oh so sublime.

Sandy beach parties begin to swirl,
With hula hoops twirling, laughter in a whirl,
A beach ball flies, a seagull reacts,
To the comedic chaos, the ocean attacks!

People do the limbo with a grin,
While local lizards just walk on in,
They judge the dancers with beady eyes,
Making bets on who will win the prize.

As the day bids farewell, the night brings cheer,
With squeals and giggles from far and near,
Iridescent moments create such mirth,
In this delightful comedy of earth!

A Symphony of Colors Above

A canvas painted in magenta and gold,
Where stories of silliness joyfully unfold,
The sun and the moon, in a playful race,
Chasing clouds at a comical pace.

A kite takes flight with a gust so strong,
It's a dance with the breeze, but not for long,
As it dips and it dives, a game of tag,
With giggles that burst from every rag.

Starfish on the shore wear a frown,
As they watch the tide roll the beach balls down,
While jellyfish waltz, twirling with grace,
Bringing whimsical joy to this vibrant place.

In this symphony where laughter rings,
And every sunset encourages wings,
The hues of humor paint the sky,
As we laugh together, oh me, oh my!

The Artistry of Evening's Palette

Colors blend with laughter's cheer,
As day bows down, the night draws near.
Brush strokes of joy, a feast of hues,
Painting the air with playful cues.

The sun slips down, a clownish glare,
Juggling clouds, without a care.
Stars pop out, like fireflies caught,
In the dance of dusk, hilarity's sought.

Tickling the breeze with silly pranks,
The moon winks bright, earning some thanks.
Silly shadows play chase and hide,
A comedy show that won't subside.

As night wraps tight in its cozy quilt,
The world's a stage, all laughter built.
With every twinkle, a chuckle's found,
In this art of night, where giggles abound.

Moonlit Serenades Over The Waves

Waves giggle gently, they're in on the jest,
A splash of humor, they surely know best.
Moonbeams chuckle on water's face,
Creating ripples in a hilarious race.

Crabs on the shore dance with delight,
Scuttling sideways, in the moon's soft light.
Fish leap out, trying to sing,
A symphony made from the joy they bring.

The night air's filled with feathery glee,
As laughter bubbles from deep in the sea.
Stars shimmy along, in a comedic spree,
Tickling the night with their bright jubilee.

Under this canvas of whimsical night,
Jokes are whispered, all feel just right.
The ocean hums a silly refrain,
As we laugh along, forgetting the strain.

Nature's Tapestry at Twilight

Nature stitches a quilt of fun,
With colors bright, as day is done.
Birds mock the sun with quirky tunes,
While frogs leap around, donning hats like loons.

Trees sway like dancers, quite absurd,
Chasing the breeze, without a word.
Critters abound, on this grand stage,
Engaging in antics that never age.

Silly scents waft on the evening air,
Flowers chuckle without a care.
Each rustle of leaves holds a pun so sweet,
In this playful paradise, life's a treat.

As daylight fades with a goofy grin,
Nature's laughter spreads beneath the skin.
Twilight's the time for the funny surprise,
In this rich tapestry, joy never dies.

Aerial Canvases of Wonder

Clouds float by, with faces aglow,
Winking at us as they drift slow.
Sunlight dances, laughing with glee,
Painting the air, wild and free.

Kites take flight, like joking friends,
Twisting and turning, the fun never ends.
Birds chirp gossip from fluffy retired,
Shooting the breeze, never tired.

The wind tells tales in whimsical ways,
An artist of jokes, spreading a haze.
Each gust a chuckle, each breeze a grin,
In this comedy sky where we all fit in.

As twilight deepens, the colors aflame,
The heavens come alive, nothing's the same.
With every twirl, the laughter falls,
In this aerial wonder, joy calls.

The Radiance of Dusk's Refrain

As sun slips down, the bugs take flight,
A squawking parrot steals my sprite.
The palm trees dance in evening's glow,
While my ice cream melts, oh no, oh no!

The beach ball rolls to meet the wave,
I dive for it, trying to be brave.
Snorkel gear seems way too tight,
A giant fish gives me a fright!

A crab approaches with a funky strut,
I laugh so hard, I think I'll bust.
Why do they walk and not just run?
Their sideways dance is such great fun!

The stars pop out, a disco show,
They twinkle, wink, and start to glow.
I sip my drink, it's quite a scene,
Chasing the dreams on a trampoline!

Island Echoes of Nightfall's Ease

The moon, a giant disco ball,
Reflects my dance, I'm feeling tall.
I trip on sand, but laugh aloud,
Even the seaweed joins the crowd.

The crickets chirp, a funny tune,
While I gaze up at the glowing moon.
A coconut falls, it hits my head,
But I just laugh and dance instead.

The gentle breeze whispers me a joke,
I giggle hard, then start to choke.
A dolphin jumps, I cheer with glee,
Who knew this night would be so free?

With every wave, the rhythm flows,
My silly moves, I can't oppose.
In this sweet spot, I feel so right,
A dance with stars, my favorite night!

Reflections of Serenity in Aerial Colors

Clouds like cotton candy float so high,
I grab a handful, and oh my, oh my!
The sun sneezes, sending rays galore,
I snicker at the sea turtles on the shore.

Laughter echoes off the waves, it's true,
A fishy face tells a joke or two.
I attempt to mimic, what a sight!
While the ocean giggles at my plight.

A kite flies by, it's shaped like cheese,
And swaying gently with the breeze.
I chase it down, my friend the crab,
As he winks at me, I can't help but blab!

The colors swirl like a watercolor book,
Nature's palette gives a playful look.
In this moment, I just can't hide,
The joy inside, it's like a wild ride!

Lifting the Veil on Celestial Secrets

Stars are gossiping up above,
Sharing secrets of the ones they love.
I peer through binoculars, what a sight,
Jupiter winks, and I giggle at night!

The constellations form silly shapes,
A turtle and socks, oh how it drapes!
An owl hoots, asks me to join,
In a funky dance, at this celestial coin.

The moon plays hide and seek with me,
Hiding behind clouds, so sly and free.
I wave at the stars, they twinkle bright,
Creating songs of pure delight!

So here I stand, under cosmic fun,
With shooting stars, I try to run.
But as I trip, I can't help but cheer,
For every tumble, brings me near!

An Ode to Lush Wonderland

In fields so green, where parrots squawk,
Loud laughter spills from every rock.
Coconuts fall like unexpected gifts,
Bouncing off heads, oh what a lift!

The monkeys swing, their antics bold,
While I play catch with a random fold.
With sand between toes, the day feels right,
Until the sun sets, turning wrong to light.

Jellyfish dance in the ocean's sway,
Whispering secrets of a beachy day.
Surfers yell as they catch a wave,
While seagulls shout, "Hey, be kind, behave!"

In this land of joy, my heart expands,
With a pineapple hat and ice-cream hands.
Where giggles chase worries far away,
In this lush wonderland, let children play!

Mirage of Colors in Heaven's Hold

The sunsets paint the clouds like a show,
While beach balls bounce, just so you know.
With laughter echoing across the sand,
Sandy snacks ready at my command!

Flip-flops flopping with every step,
While crabs perform a sideways prep.
Colorful drinks with umbrellas so small,
Pretend they're castles, we'll have a ball!

The stars above twinkle and tease,
Like pixies whispering in the breeze.
But fireflies are the real VIPs,
Dancing around like they own the trees!

In a mirage of colors, life's all a game,
Where each giggle feels totally lame.
Yet here in this land, we just can't resist,
A mash-up of fun that'll always persist!

Breath of Warmth in the Twilight Air

The twilight giggles, it knows a muse,
As crickets sing blues with sandalwood shoes.
A warm breeze teases my unruly hair,
While buzzing bugs play hide and share!

Under palm trees, we weave silly tales,
Of mermaids, pirates, and inflatable whales.
The moon's a giant marshmallow tonight,
We roast our dreams as we bask in the light.

A friendly crab tries to steal my shoe,
Laughing along just like a kooky view.
With frosty drinks that sparkles and fizz,
We toast to weirdness, and that's how it is!

As night unfolds with a wink and a grin,
Every little giggle invites us back in.
Breath in the warmth, let worries take flight,
For in this silliness, all feels just right!

Celestial Echoes over the Canopy

Up in the trees, where the owls chat,
Echoes of laughter from a playful cat.
Bubbles float up, in a sly little dance,
While friends chase shadows, lost in a trance.

The stars poke fun in the velvety night,
Whispering secrets, oh what a sight!
Koalas giggle as they munch on leaves,
Telling tall tales that no one believes.

Crickets on stages, performers of sound,
Juggling their tunes all around.
With every chirp, the laughter grows,
In a concert of joy, anything goes!

So we raise our glasses to the bizarre,
To friendship and laughter, near and far.
With celestial echoes, we find our way,
In a canopy of giggles, let's forever play!

The Serenade of Exotic Nights

Under twinkling stars we play,
With dancing shadows all around,
A parrot sings a quirky tune,
While mongooses spin and bound.

Coconuts drop with a thud,
As laughter echoes through the trees,
The crickets join our merry song,
While monkeys swing with little ease.

A frog croaks what he thinks is gold,
But all we hear is silly glee,
In the coolness of the night,
We toast with drinks made from sweet tea.

So grab a hat and join the fun,
The night is young, the moon's our guide,
We'll dance until the morning sun,
In this wild and joyful ride.

Heavenly Canopies of Fragrant Blooms

Bees are buzzing, flowers sway,
The sweet scent carries us away,
A butterfly slips on a shoe,
And lands right on the fragrant brew.

The daisies laugh, they twist and twirl,
While tulips blush and start to unfurl,
A squirrel performs acrobatics fine,
As clouds giggle, drinking sunshine.

The pigeons strut, with such bravado,
While a dog tries to dance the cha-cha,
But alas, he trips, what a sight!
He dreams of joining in the flight.

With colors bright, the day's a feast,
Of giggles, blooms, a happy beast,
So let's all waltz through gardens wide,
Where humor blooms and laughter's tied.

Chasing Clouds in Paradise

We chased a cloud, oh what a race,
It giggled and puffed, oh what a face!
With cotton candy dreams so light,
We jumped so high, oh what a sight!

The sun peeked down, he tossed a wink,
As jellyfish in the air did sink,
Umbrellas soared like flying fish,
A clownfish danced, fulfilling a wish.

A hammock swung with a gentle creak,
As we sought fun, week after week,
But then the cloud, it burst with laughter,
We splashed below, oh what a disaster!

Yet through it all, we never frown,
Instead, we prance, we twirl around,
With rainbows bright, our hearts will sing,
In this world of joy, we are the kings!

The Dance of Light on the Sea

Waves roll in with a glimmering grin,
The sun holds hands with the ocean's spin,
Fish in tuxedos swim with flair,
While seaweed waves like it just don't care.

A crab tries to moonwalk on the sand,
While seagulls cheer, it's all quite grand,
A dolphin jumps in a sparkling dive,
"We're here to party!" they seem to jive.

The beach ball bounces, a comical clash,
As toddlers tumble, oh what a splash,
The tide pulls in a picnic feast,
With sandwiches shared by the feathery beast.

Under the sun's jovial charm,
Let's dance where light brings no alarm,
For in this world of whimsy and fun,
Our laughter sparkles, we're never done!

Harmonies Above in Paradise

In a land where the sun wears shades,
Palm trees dance in hula parades.
Coconuts drop with a boisterous thunk,
The birds all squawk, they're never a funk.

A monkey swings by, wearing a hat,
Mocks the tourist, and that's all of that.
He steals a snack and gives a loud cheer,
Then bounces away—oh, where's he gone here?

The waves laugh and tumble in glee,
A crab styles its hair quite fashionably.
Seagulls squawk jokes, trading puns,
While lounging beachgoers soak up the fun.

With flip-flops clapping like a drum,
Everyone's dancing, they can't help but hum.
A parrot tells tales that are rarely true,
In paradise, laughter is always the view.

The Enchantment of Vibrant Horizons

The sun pops up like toast on a plate,
Brightening worlds—oh, isn't it great?
Umbrellas blossom in colors so fine,
While shops sell mango shakes divine.

A juggler drops coconuts, oh what a sight,
Kids giggle and yell, 'That's not quite right!'
Pirates sing songs that are way off-key,
But who cares? They're there to set us all free.

Hula dancers spin and whirl with flair,
Chasing the tourists and tossing their hair.
While fish in the sea hide from the sun,
They gossip about who's the most fun.

As shadows grow long and the sunset beams,
The horizon bursts forth in candy-like dreams.
With laughter around, it's a festival scene,
In this vibrant world, everyone's a queen!

Whispers of the Ocean Breeze

The breeze teases waves like a playful friend,
Telling tales of turtles who never pretend.
Seashells chuckle, playing peek-a-boo,
In a world of laughter, there's always something new.

Fishermen wave with their nets in a twist,
Hoping for fish, yet getting the mist.
With a wink and a grin, they share a laugh,
Claiming their catch was a dolphin's giraffe.

Sandcastles tumble with a mighty roar,
Kids shout with joy before building once more.
And when a wave crashes, they squeal like cats,
Running in circles, dodging the splats.

The sun takes a bow as the day fades out,
While crabs on the shore know there's never doubt.
With giggles and chuckles under the moon's tease,
The ocean keeps whispering sweet, silly pleas.

Celestial Canopy of Dreams

Stars sprinkle laughter from way up high,
While clouds make shapes of a dog or a pie.
Fireflies wink, playing tag in the night,
And crickets compose sweet tunes with delight.

A frog croaks jokes from his lily pad throne,
Claiming that croaking is better alone.
But the fish all giggle, swimming below,
As the moonlight sparkles like glittering snow.

The breeze rustles leaves, sharing tales of the day,
While owls hoot softly, 'Let's dance and play!'
Even the nighttime is filled with surprise,
In this canopy where wonder never dies.

As clouds drift on by, in whimsical waltz,
Each twinkling star has its own quirky pulse.
With laughter and dreams floating so free,
The night in this world is pure jubilee.

An Ode to the Southern Cross

In the night, stars are winking,
Making jokes while we're thinking.
The sky, a vast giggle fest,
With lights that urge us to jest.

Beneath the twinkle, I lie flat,
Listen to a chattering bat.
'Knock, knock!' shouts the spinning orb,
While shooting stars join in the blurb.

A big dipper steals the show,
With funny faces in a row.
As laughter fills the cosmic space,
Even the moon wears a silly face.

So here I am, a bemused host,
To glowing friends I love the most.
In this humor-filled expanse,
I can't help but laugh and dance.

Night's Tranquility Over Serene Waters

Floating dreams on a silver stream,
Fish are giggling, or so it seems.
The water whispers jokes and sighs,
While frogs perform in a great reprise.

Turtles floating, taking bets,
On splashy shows with no regrets.
A sleepy owl cracks open a pun,
As moons play tag and have some fun.

Ripples dance like giggling sprites,
With laughter echoing through the nights.
The crickets chirp with teasing rhymes,
In this tranquil world where joy climbs.

As waves play tunes of frothy glee,
I chuckle at the antics, you see.
Beneath the cloak of softest shade,
The night's a comic serenade.

Variegated Layers of Twilight

Colors blend like pranks at play,
Sunset giggles brighten the day.
Clouds are artists, what a show!
Painting hues from head to toe.

A tangerine with hints of blue,
Poking fun at the still, clear view.
It waves goodbye with a cheeky grin,
As stars emerge with a silly spin.

The horizon yawns, stretching wide,
As night-time jokers gear up to ride.
Midnight orchestrates a grand parade,
Where shadows chuckle and mischief's made.

In this canvas, laughter flourishes,
Each flickering star warmly nourishes.
So raise a toast to twilight's grace,
With every hue brings a happy face.

A Celestial Symphony of Waves

Bubbles rise with a giggling sound,
While the ocean shares puns all around.
Seashells chuckle as surfers glide,
On the foamy front, where mischief hides.

The tide sets up a snappy beat,
As fish join in for the funny treat.
Water spouts with joyful glee,
Making waves that dance with me.

Mermaids toss jokes from the deep,
Waking sailors from their sleep.
Starfish rolling in laughter's game,
Under the moon's playful name.

In this concert of sea and sky,
Clap your hands, let the humor fly.
A symphony where delight flows,
Through every wave, the laughter grows.

Lush Hues of Daybreak

Morning blooms with colors bright,
Parrots squawking, what a sight!
Coffee spills upon my shirt,
Laughter hides beneath the mirth.

Sunshine dances, grass goes boom,
I trip over a peacock plume.
Nature's brush, a playful tease,
Watch me stumble with such ease!

Palm trees sway in silly glee,
A monkey swings and shouts at me.
Flip-flops flying, oh what fun,
A morning's mess has just begun!

Joyous moments, come what may,
In this wild, bright, sunny play.
With every fall, I'll cheer and grin,
Tomorrow's clumsiness begins again!

Ethereal Embrace of Sunset and Sea

The sun dips down in hues of red,
I chase a crab, can't feel my legs!
A splash, a laugh, it's quite a sight,
I blame the ocean for my plight.

Flip-flops lost beneath the wave,
I ponder if I'm just a knave.
The gulls giggle, oh what class,
They mock my dance, I run, alas!

Warm winds tease my tousled hair,
A sunset's beauty, but beware!
My sandwich flies, a seagull's treat,
In this seaside tale, I'm beat.

But as the sky begins to fade,
I'll raise a toast to the charade.
For every splash and giggle here,
Life's funny moments, give a cheer!

Stars that Wink Beneath the Breeze

Under a blanket of sparkling night,
I trip on sand, oh what a fright!
Stars above, they twinkle and tease,
I tussle with a playful breeze.

That coconut fell from a high tree,
Just like my sense of dignity!
The moon laughs, a big old moon,
We're dancing here, a silly tune.

With every breeze, a funny smell,
Did the fish just wish me well?
Stars are winking, can't you see?
Or is it just an eye on me?

Yet in this chaos, joy abounds,
Laughter echoes, silly sounds.
With each misstep, my heart's embrace,
In this odd dance, I've found my place!

Celestial Choreography Above

Clouds parade in fluffy rows,
I try to ride them, off it goes!
A kite's entangled in my hair,
The sky's a stage, I'm unaware.

Each bird flutters, appears to strut,
While I just trip and hit a rut.
The sun, a spotlight, bright and loud,
As I perform, I feel quite proud.

Waves of laughter, more than grace,
I tumble down, forget my place.
Stars applaud, with twinkling cheer,
In this mishap, I have no fear.

So let the cosmos dance away,
While I swirl in a silly play.
For every fall, there's laughter sure,
Life's celestial ways are quite the cure!

Dawn's Embrace Over Coral Reefs

The sun's a clumsy painter, it spills bright hues,
With tangled beams, it stumbles and it skews.
Fish wear sunglasses, they flip and dive,
While crabs try breakdancing, feeling alive.

An octopus in flip-flops, feeling so fly,
Waves crash like jokes, oh my, oh my!
Seashells giggle, the ocean's their stage,
Seaweed is dancing, full of youthful rage.

The seagulls squawk in silly rhymes,
They steal your chips with perfect crimes.
Flamingos prance, in tutus they strut,
All saying, "Hey, don't take life too cut!"

As dawn breaks softly, waves know their part,
Nature's own comedy, a work of art.
In this cheeky paradise, laughter takes flight,
Where morning's embrace brings joy and delight.

Sunlit Palms and Endless Horizons

Under swaying palms, the squirrels all chatter,
They've got a talent for playful patter.
Monkeys juggling coconuts, what a display,
Each nut they drop means laughter on the way.

A toucan in shades gives the world a glance,
His bright beak, the style, brings birds to dance.
Cocktails with umbrellas line the shore,
Waiting for someone to spill the score.

The sun's like a kid, splashing in pools,
While crabs play poker, breaking all the rules.
With endless horizons that tickle the mind,
Adventure whispers, "See what you can find!"

Even the turtles are feeling quite bold,
Racing each other like stories untold.
In this sunlit paradise, laughter's the key,
As joy drifts along, wild and free!

Azure Tides and Stars Aligned

The waves giggle softly, tickling the shore,
While starfish debate on who's keeping score.
Seashells in gossip, swirling their tales,
Conch shells proclaiming fishy details.

The moon is a joker, shines goofy and bright,
Pulling the tides like it's a funny sight.
Dolphins perform, in leaps and in bounds,
Splashing out laughter, the best kind of sounds.

Crabs in tuxedos sway side to side,
Under the stars, they dance with pride.
Jellyfish disco in luminescent splendor,
While sea urchins lounge, feeling the tender.

With each wave, a chuckle, a fizz, a pop,
The ocean's a stage, where wonders don't stop.
In this azure realm, joy reigns supreme,
With laughter and light, we float on the dream.

Vibrant Canvases of Dusk

When shadows grow long, the colors collide,
Pineapples wear crowns, taking fun in stride.
Fireflies host parties with their little lights,
While the crickets join in, on summer nights.

Painting with laughter, the dusk spreads wide,
Tropical pies riddle, who'll take the ride?
Bananas in pajamas, all snug in their beds,
While playful parakeets spin tales in their heads.

As waves wash ashore with a silly splash,
The sky throws confetti, a colorful cache.
Palm trees are giggling, they sway and groove,
Making up dances, in the tropical move.

In vibrant hues, where fun intertwines,
The sunset's a canvas for silly designs.
With each fleeting moment, joy blurs the line,
In this realm of laughter, the stars brightly shine.

Driftwood Under Velvet Skies

Driftwood lounges, looking quite chill,
Caught in a breeze, it dreams of a thrill.
Stars peer down, giggling in rows,
While crabs on the beach gossip in tows.

A seagull squawks, 'Why don't you float?',
Driftwood just grins, 'I'm not a boat!'
With waves that tease and tickle so nice,
It leans back and sips ocean ice.

The moon takes a nap, snuggled in sand,
Driftwood declares, 'This is so grand!'
As fish throw a party, all fins in the air,
The night whispers, 'Come join if you dare!'

So here on the shore, life takes a spin,
Driftwood chuckles, 'Let the fun begin!'
With laughter that echoes through night's playful might,
Nature's own joke, under soft silver light.

Coral Dreams in Celestial Light

Under water, colors dance with zest,
Coral giggles, 'We're at our best!'
Fish wear bow ties, strutting with flair,
While squids pull pranks with ink in the air.

A turtle dreams of a time he was fast,
But now he just swims, lost in the past.
'Oh, to be young!' he sighs with a frown,
While jellyfish giggle, floating around.

Starfish hold parties, on rocks wave and sway,
Inviting the seaweed to join in the fray.
Crabs click their claws like they're keeping the beat,
A conch shell plays tunes, oh, what a treat!

Coral chuckles, 'Why so serious, guys?'
With each passing wave, laughter surely flies.
In dreams made of bubbles, joy's always in sight,
As they twirl under beams of the soft, celestial light.

Palm Fronds Whispering Secrets

Palm fronds gossip in the warm, soft breeze,
'Have you heard the news? It's all over the seas!'
They flutter and fan with a cheeky delight,
Sprinkling the sun with tales of the night.

A lizard scurries, wearing shades of green,
Trying to blend in, but it's quite the scene!
The palm trees chuckle, their leaves play at dance,
While crickets serenade, hoping for a chance.

In the shade, there's a party, oh what a sight,
With squirrels and raccoons, all dressed up tight.
'Hurry up, come!' the palm fronds implore,
'Join our mad tea party, you'll never feel bored!'

The sun sinks low, dressing all in gold,
And all of the palms, they giggle and fold.
Whispers of laughter, secrets collide,
In the arms of the palms, where fun cannot hide.

Sunkissed Reflections on Still Waters

On still waters, the sun wears a grin,
It flirts with the waves, inviting them in.
Frogs trade their croaks for a splash and a dive,
While ducks crack jokes, feeling so alive.

A fish, with a splash, throws a water balloon,
While the turtles just laugh, basking in noon.
Sunkissed reflections ripple and sway,
They dance on the surface, come join in the play!

The dragonflies zoom, like they own the place,
Whispering secrets with grace and with pace.
'Why so serious?' they tease as they twirl,
While the pond takes a sip, letting time unfurl.

So here on the edge, where sunlight does glow,
Joy bounces lightly, with nary a woe.
Sunkissed giggles float out to delight,
As the waters reflect every laugh through the night.

A Feathered Canvas Woven by Nature

In a jungle, birds gossip with flair,
Painting gossip in colorful air.
A parrot declares it's a fashion show,
While a toucan laughs, saying, "Who stole the glow?"

Monkeys in sunglasses swing with style,
Chasing each other in a chattering file.
A sloth shimmies, though it's quite slow,
Declaring it's just taking it easy, you know!

Bright flowers join in with a vibrant cheer,
"Wear me today, make a splash here!"
A bee buzzes loudly, stealing the scene,
While a snail whispers, "This party's just keen!"

The stars above twinkle and tease,
As the moon leans in, laughing with ease.
Saying, "Nature's the best at creating this fun,
Let's dance till the dawn, oh, everyone!"

Tranquil Rhythms of the Ocean's Lullaby

Waves tumble in, giggling with glee,
As crabs do the cha-cha, quite carefree.
Seagulls squawk jokes while gliding on high,
While fish play poker, hiding nearby.

The tide rolls in with a sneaky grin,
Whispers to shells, "Shall we begin?"
A dolphin snickers at a dive too bold,
While a clam grumbles, "I'm just too cold!"

A beach ball bounces, provoking a race,
As flip-flops fly all over the place.
Sandcastles topple with a royal decree,
"Long live the king of the sand and the sea!"

The sun sets down, painting laughter in hue,
As starfish applaud the curtain of dew.
Each wave bows out with a comedy call,
Reminding all beachgoers to enjoy it all!

Celestial Treasures in Lush Gardens

Butterflies flutter, a comedic parade,
Wearing bright colors that can't quite fade.
"Look at my wings!" a monarch boasts,
While a moth chimes in, "I'm popular, the most!"

The flowers giggle, each bloom in delight,
Who's the prettiest? They argue all night.
A sunflower shrugs, "I'm tall, you see!"
While daisies dare, "We're just full of glee!"

Bees buzz a tune, drumming up cheer,
As ants march in lines, saying, "We're here!"
A mole pops up, his hat slightly askew,
"Who wants to join in? The garden's a zoo!"

Stars twinkle down, winking with glee,
As night falls in, inviting a spree.
"Let's dance with the moon, oh joyous delight!"
In this lush garden, laughter takes flight!

Warm Breezes and Distant Horizons

A warm breeze whispered, "What's the scoop?"
While palm trees swayed, forming a troupe.
"Let's play frisbee!" the coconuts said,
As a dog chased its tail, nearly falling ahead.

Flip-flops flopped with a rhythm so fine,
As children built castles, plotting to dine.
A crab slides by on its sideways quest,
"Who needs a suit? I'm dressed to impress!"

Kites tangle above, a colorful mess,
As giggles burst forth, no need to impress.
A lizard does yoga on a sun-warmed stone,
While a frog croaks, "I feel quite alone!"

As daylight recedes, fireflies ignite,
Saying, "Join our dance, it's quite a sight!"
Laughter and joy unite in the night,
In warmth, we roam, under stars shining bright!

The Essence of Nightfall's Charm

As shadows stretch on sandy shores,
The crabs declare their crabby wars.
A coconut falls with a hefty thud,
As seagulls giggle at a slimy dud.

Bananas sway in the evening breeze,
Whispering secrets to the buzzing bees.
The moon wears shades, looking quite grand,
While fish dance on land, oh isn't it planned?

Frogs croak jokes in a raucous way,
A turtle plays cards, saying, "Just one more play!"
Laughter echoes through the dusky scene,
In this oddball world, where nothing's routine.

The stars take bets on who will dive first,
A starfish insists he can quench his thirst!
Nightfall's charm, a comedic delight,
Underneath the moon, everything feels right.

Spheres of Light in Paradise

In the hammock, a sloth snoozes tight,
His dreams involve a daring kite flight.
Fish in the pond wear hats made of leaves,
While a lizard does ballet, oh what a tease!

Mangoes drop like disco balls,
As parrots throw shade, making funny calls.
The sun dips low, like it's running late,
Time for a party, don't contemplate!

Glow worms flicker in a dance so spry,
While a turtle munches on a slice of pie.
Fireflies buzz with a flickering grin,
In this realm of joy, where chuckles begin.

Clouds parade as fluffy white ships,
Acting as comedians with silly quips.
Light in the air, laughter all around,
Spheres of joy in paradise abound.

Whirling Flora Amidst Celestial Lights

The flowers sway, doing the twist,
A dandelion joins, not wanting to miss.
Bees do the cha-cha, full of flare,
While petals compete for the sweetest pair.

A vine climbs high, whispering jokes,
Entertaining the clumps of chatting folks.
Tulips gossip, while daisies laugh loud,
It's a floral fiesta, bright and proud.

The sunbeam slides in with a goofy grin,
Saying, "Let's lose ourselves, let the fun begin!"
Planets peek down, giggling with glee,
At this garden party, full of harmony.

With a flip and a twirl, all join the fun,
Underneath the rays of the setting sun.
In this realm where flora takes flight,
Whirling together, under the starlit night.

Drift in the Day's Fading Glow

As daylight takes a tiptoe bow,
The fish parade, caught in a wow.
An octopus wears a fancy hat,
While a dolphin dances with a lazy cat.

Palm trees sway, feeling quite bold,
Baker crabs sell pastries, plenty to hold.
A sunset's wink, painting skies anew,
While laughter spreads like a warm sea view.

Shrimp join hands, making a chain,
Singing silly songs that make you untrain.
Under the blush of a rosy blend,
The fun never stops, our heartfelt mend.

Glow of the evening, laughter ignites,
As we drift in the glow of playful nights.
Each moment shines, like glitter, like gold,
In these fading hours, let your joy unfold.

Starlit Secrets of the Southern Hemisphere

Beneath the moon, we dance on sand,
With piña coladas held in hand.
A crab joins in, doing the twist,
His sideways shuffle can't be missed.

A parrot squawks, giving us sass,
While dodging waves, we all fall down fast.
The stars above, a glittery show,
Let's hope that dolphin won't steal the flow!

The fireflies giggle, lighting the scene,
While someone's bathing in sunscreen sheen.
A coconut drops, a comical thud,
We cheer for the fruit that now is our bud.

Toasted marshmallows taste divine,
But watch your eyebrows near the fire's line.
With sand in our shoes and joy in our hearts,
We laugh at the night, it's just full of smarts!

Sunlit Vistas and Moonlit Tales

In daylight bright, we drink our tea,
While a monkey swings from a palm so free.
He steals the snack; we just laugh with glee,
Guess who's winning this game of spree?

The ice cream cone tops our fun parade,
Dripping quickly in the sun's hot shade.
A seagull swoops, it's quite the charade,
It guzzles our treat—what a rogue brigade!

As twilight falls and shadows creep,
We share our secrets, promise to keep.
The stars above begin to peep,
While crickets sing us sweet tunes to sleep.

But wait, is that a squirrel in shades?
We giggle hard at the antics played.
Under moonlight's gaze, the world's a delight,
Join the wild laughter, it's a silly night!

The Palette of an Endless Summer

The sun blares loud, colors collide,
With beach balls flying, oh what a ride!
A flip-flop lost bounces by the tide,
While laughter rolls like the waves worldwide.

We paint our toes in neon hues,
While dodging splashes from sandy shoes.
A clam sings out with corny clues,
Our beach day's bright, with nothing to lose!

As twilight dawns, sparklers ignite,
We roast marshmallows, oh what a sight!
The glow of the coast in fading light,
Even the seashells seem to feel just right.

And who's that dancing with a hat made of gold?
We wink and we jest as the night unfolds.
Under the stars, we draw with glee,
Creating a canvas of memories free!

Dreaming Under the Canopy of Coral

Under ocean waves, we bob and weave,
Corals whisper secrets, if you believe.
A fish in tuxedo takes his leave,
While others giggle at tricks they achieve.

The jellyfish glide, look so fine,
Dressed in colors from a rainbow design.
One tries to dance, oh how divine,
But who knew dancing could be so malign?

The mermaids laugh, sharing their jokes,
While sea turtles race past fragrant oaks.
We join their games, biting our hoax,
"Who's faster?" we cheer, amid all the pokes.

As twilight arrives, with lanterns aglow,
We hum silly tunes, our spirits in tow.
In this wild dream where fun can't stall,
We dive into laughter, and that's the best call!

www.ingramcontent.com/pod-product-compliance
Lightning Source LLC
Chambersburg PA
CBHW072130070526
44585CB00016B/1608